Bygone CLYDEBANK

by
John Hood

Until its closure in the late 1970s, the most prominent building at Clydebank Cross was Arthur Booth's (later Eric Hutcheon's) popular Clydebank Bar. Less popular perhaps was George Campbell's Dental Surgery which occupied premises above the bar. One of several dental surgeries in the vicinity of the Cross, on its opening in 1911 it advertised that 'first class workmanship [was] guaranteed'. Among the traders on the north side of Dumbarton Road was a fish and chip shop and, at No. 20, the Bank of Scotland. Following a merger of the Bank of Scotland and the Commercial Bank of Scotland in 1959, it was decided to close the Commercial Bank's branch in nearby Glasgow Road, and concentrate the operations of the newly named National Commercial Bank of Scotland in their Dumbarton Road branch. At that time, the premises were modernised and extended. All of the buildings seen here were demolished in the 1970s.

First published in the United Kingdom, 2005,
reprinted 2012
by Stenlake Publishing Ltd.
01290 551122
www.stenlake.co.uk

ISBN 978-1-84033-350-3

**The publishers regret that they cannot supply
copies of any pictures featured in this book.**

FURTHER READING

The books listed below were used by the author during his research. None of them are available from Stenlake Publishing. Those interested in finding out more are advised to contact their local bookshop or reference library.

A.W. Brotchie and R.L. Grieves, *Dumbarton's Trams and Buses*, Dundee: N.B. Traction, 1985.
John Hood (compiler), *The History of Clydebank*, Carnforth: Parthenon Press, 1988.
John Hood, *Clydebank in Old Picture Postcards*, Zaltbommel: European Library, 1985.
John Thomas, *Regional History of Railways, Vol. 6: Scotland*, Newton Abbot: David and
    Charles, 1971.

ACKNOWLEDGEMENTS

I would like to thank the following people for their help: Gerry Agnew, Robert D. Laidlaw, Mary Frances McGlynn, Wallace McIntyre, the McEwen family and Jimmy Ward. In particular, I would like to thank Pat Malcolm for comments on the manuscript.

On a dull, grey Sunday afternoon in June 1931, thousands gathered in and around Hall Street, Clydebank. Some, in accordance with the old Scottish tradition, 'hung oot the windaes' of nearby tenements, all to witness the official unveiling of the Clydebank War Memorial by the Lord Lieutenant of Dunbartonshire, Sir Iain Colquhoun of Luss. The War Memorial, part of which was designed in the form of a Greek 'pylon' or temple entrance, was incorporated into the base of the Clydebank Town Hall bell tower. Designed by architect James Miller (who had also designed Clydebank Town Hall itself), the memorial stood eighteen and a half feet high and was built of pearl-grey Northumberland stone and polished black marble. The bronze figure representing peace, which forms the centrepiece of the memorial, is seven feet tall, and was the work of Londoner Walter Gilbert. When the memorial was officially unveiled, a four-faced clock and a carillon of eight bells (both intended to form part of the memorial) had already been in place for over a year.

INTRODUCTION

The origins of Clydebank can be traced back to 1 May 1871 when local landowner Miss Grace Hamilton cut the first turf for a new shipyard being built on the farmlands of West Barns o' Clyde. The shipyard was owned by James and George Thomson, who were having to vacate the site of their shipyard upriver at Govan, as this was required for the construction of Princes Dock. Clydebank Shipyard (as the yard was known) initially provided employment for several hundred workers. In addition, the Thomsons erected tenements alongside the new shipyard to house their workers, and allowed the use of shipyard bothies for educational, religious and social purposes. Perhaps it is not surprising, then, that initially the small but growing community around the shipyard was often referred to as 'Tamson's Toon'. The later arrival in the area of the Singer Manufacturing Company, who began construction of what would eventually become the largest sewing machine factory in Europe, provided further impetus to the local economy. These two major employers acted as a magnet to sundry smaller businesses. This growth in the local economy encouraged several prominent local businessmen to seek elevation of the community into a Police Burgh. One of the most influential of these was the then co-owner of the Clydebank Shipyard, James Rodger Thomson, so it was perhaps no real surprise that when the town was raised to the status of a Police Burgh on 18 November 1886, he was elected the town's first provost. The new burgh was officially named Clydebank.

Thereafter, Clydebank experienced such a rate of growth in population that it gained 'Tamson's Toon' the new title of 'the risingest burgh'. This also encouraged a dramatic increase in the provision of good affordable workmen's houses, first by employers such as Thomson's, and later by independent builders, such as J.W. Anderson, Robert McAlpine and Leslie Kirk. Associated with population growth was, of course, the need to provide for the religious, educational and social welfare of the inhabitants. Here again, employers such as the Thomsons and Singer displayed a benevolent attitude to their workers' needs. Both Clydebank's first church (the 'Tarry Kirk') and its first school (the 'Bothy School') were located within Clydebank Shipyard, while Singer (and to a lesser extent Thomson's), provided extensive recreational and social facilities for their workers and their families.

There was also a marked improvement in transport infrastructure: by 1896, Clydebank was served by not one, but three, separate railway lines, all competing fiercely for a share of the lucrative and ever-increasing freight and passenger traffic. In addition, by 1903, Clydebank had a tramway system.

Indeed, the economic and population growth in the area was such that eventually the Police Burgh outgrew the boundaries which had been set in 1886. However, despite constant pressure from 1890 onwards by the Commissioners (who managed the Police Burgh's affairs), it was not until 1906 that the burgh boundaries were expanded to include Radnor Park. Further extensions were then authorised in 1925, 1937, 1949 and finally in 1975, at which time a comprehensive re-organisation of local government in Scotland resulted in the demise of Clydebank Burgh Council and its replacement by a new and expanded Clydebank District Council.

Although the boundary extensions had provided the local authority with much-needed land for development, the momentum which had once fuelled the local economy had, by the mid-1950s, slowed down considerably. Ultimately, a series of factory closures led to massive job losses, perhaps the most significant being the closure of John Brown and Company in 1972, and the closure of Singer in 1980. The scale of the job losses, however, led to Clydebank being chosen as the site for Scotland's first Enterprise Zone in 1981. The last three decades have also seen Clydebank being served by a regional shopping centre, and the opening of a state-of-the-art hospital. In 1996, a further re-organisation of local boundaries led to a merger of Clydebank and Dumbarton District Councils to form the new West Dunbartonshire Council.

One very sad chapter of Clydebank's history which will live on in the memory of Bankies for years to come is the events of the nights of 13 and 14 March 1941, known as the 'Clydebank Blitz', when Clydebank was targeted by German bombers. The attacks left over 500 people dead and many injured. Large swathes of Clydebank were left in ruins. In fact, all but seven of the burgh's 12,000 houses were damaged. Ordinary people showed courage and strength in the face of adversity and many received awards for their bravery.

I hope that the many images reproduced within this book will rekindle memories and help to ensure that Clydebank's history is not forgotten.

In this 1962 photograph, a Glasgow Corporation Coronation tram and, to its left, a smaller single-deck 'special' tram, are making their way along Dumbarton Road. The tenements stretching from the Town Hall to the extreme right of the picture were known locally as Brown's Buildings, and were erected *c.*1916 by shipbuilders John Brown and Company. During the Clydebank Blitz in 1941 some of the tenements were damaged, resulting in a gap site, which lay empty until the late 1980s, when new tenements were erected. Brown's Buildings continued to be owned by John Brown and Company until the late 1970s, when ownership was transferred to Clydebank District Council. On 7 December 1989, one of the tenements, after renovation by the owners, Clydebank Housing Association, was officially re-opened and named the John Rannie Building in memory of a former Clydebank Shipyard director. The garage to the left of the picture was for many years owned by Clydebank Motors. In 1950 the premises were taken over by John Weddell and Victor Devine, who also operated from showrooms at the corner of Dumbarton Road and Miller Street.

On 9 May 1910, after much debate, Clydebank Town Council accepted an offer by Dunfermline-born philanthropist Andrew Carnegie of £10,000 to fund the building of a public library. For its part, the Council was required to provide a suitable site and sufficient funds to maintain the new service. The resultant new Carnegie Library, seen here shortly after its opening on 1 October 1913, was built on Dumbarton Road on ground acquired from John Brown and Company. The building was designed in the classical style by Messrs Gardner, Miller and White. There was provision on the ground floor for lending and reference departments, a magazine room and a newsroom, while staffrooms and a bookstore were located within the basement. The upper floor housed a students' room, in addition to the Librarian's private living quarters. This flat was accessed separately from a ground-floor entrance on the library's western gable. Although the library was built alongside the already existing Morison Memorial Church, for some reason the church has been blanked out of this particular picture!

When this photograph was taken around 1909, an unbroken row of tenements still lined both sides of Dumbarton Road, stretching from Miller Street (on the left) to Clydebank Cross. At the entrance to Miller Street is Ross's Bar, which was owned by John (and later James) Gibb Ross. It was sold about 1960 to a local firm, McGown and Cameron, and renamed the Burgh Bar. The bar closed down in the late 1960s, when the tenement it was housed in was demolished. Further along in Miller Street were the Temperance Hotel, the Clydebank Higher Grade School and, from 1941 to the late 1960s, McGoldrick's dairy. The McGoldricks opened their first shop in Clydebank in 1912, in John Knox Street, but relocated to Miller Street after the dairy was hit by a landmine during the Clydebank Blitz. In the late 1960s, when the shop at 14 Miller Street was acquired by compulsory purchase, the dairy moved again – this time around the corner to Dumbarton Road, where it remained until the tenements were demolished. In all, the McGoldrick family were in business in Clydebank for 62 years.

By the late 1930s, the stretch of Dumbarton Road seen here from Clydebank Cross to the 'Caley' bridge had been fully developed. The bridge had been built to carry the former Caledonian Railway line across Dumbarton Road, hence 'Caley' bridge. During the Clydebank Blitz of March 1941, some of the tenements on the left were damaged. However, it was the developer's axe that later felled those on the right at Adelaide Place. One structure that did survive both the Blitz and redevelopment was the winged figure of Mercury, seen here atop Clydebank Town Hall bell tower. Mercury, more popularly known as 'the Angel', is said to have adorned one of the pavilions at the 1901 Glasgow International Exhibition, before being used by James Miller to ornament the bell tower. There it remained until 1968, when it was toppled by a severe January storm. When it fell the statue broke in three, but happily was later repaired by John Brown Engineering's Brass Shop personnel. It was then mounted on a wooden plinth and repositioned within the main foyer of Clydebank Town Hall, where it remains to this day.

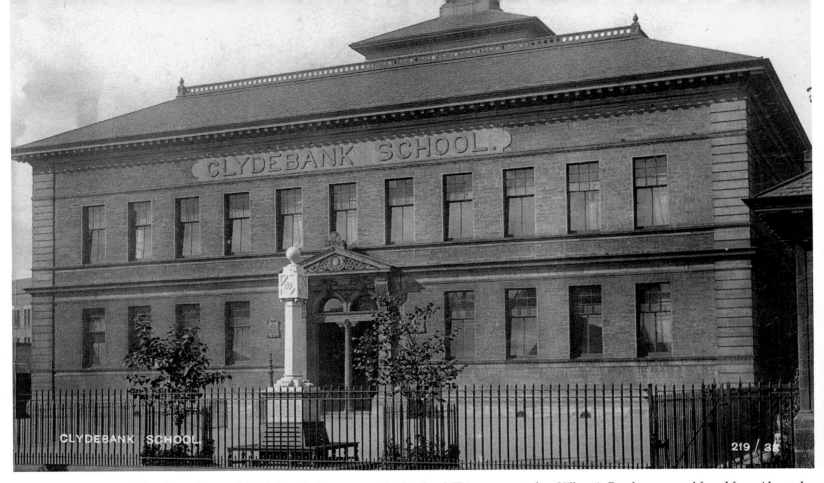

In 1876 Old Kilpatrick School Board opened Clydebank's first purpose-built school. This was erected on Kilbowie Road, on ground feued from Alexander Dunn Pattison. But barely ten years later, work had begun on a larger, more lavish replacement. This was opened on 4 February 1888 by Sir John Neilson Cuthbertson, Chairman of the Glasgow School Board. Built on the site of the original school, at a cost of £20,000 (£7,000 above budget), the new school was considered locally to be an extravagance. Angry ratepayers took to the streets in protest and burnt an effigy of the Old Kilpatrick School Board Chairman, the Rev. John Stark. Also seen, within the school playground, is a slender grey granite hexagonal memorial. This was erected in 1910 by friends of the late Dr James Stevenson, Medical Officer of Health for the Burgh of Clydebank from 1897 to 1909. Dr Stevenson, a former Chairman of the Old Kilpatrick School Board, had been a passionate advocate of education and it was thought appropriate that his memorial should be sited within the school grounds.

In 1906, Clydebank School on Kilbowie Road was elevated to the status of a Higher Grade school with two distinct divisions, that of Primary and Post-Primary. Although the school had originally been designed to cope with up to 1,500 pupils (excluding Technical students), a fast-increasing school roll forced Old Kilpatrick School Board to provide additional accommodation to the rear of the school in Miller Street. The new annexe (seen here) was opened on 2 November 1911 by the Chairman of the School Board, the Rev. Thomas M. McKendrick. The two buildings jointly became Clydebank High School around 1921, although the annexe continued to be referred to locally as Clydebank Higher Grade School. During the Clydebank Blitz, the annexe was slightly damaged, but continued to operate until 1947, when pupils transferred to the new Clydebank High School in Janetta Street. After that the annexe served a multitude of roles, before it was demolished in the early 1980s.

In May 1897, when the Glasgow, Yoker and Clydebank railway line was extended to Dalmuir, a station (shown here) was opened with access from Alexander Street. This new station was initially called Clydebank (later Clydebank Central) and the original terminus at Whitecrook Street (which had been called Clydebank) was renamed Clydebank East. At one time there were no fewer than five railway lines traversing Clydebank, which inevitably led to town planning becoming somewhat fragmented. It also impacted on other forms of transport, such as the use of single-deck trams on the Clydebank–Duntocher route, due to height restrictions. Even today, the height of the railway bridge across Kilbowie Road constantly poses problems for buses and high-sided vehicles.

In 1906, the original Kilbowie Station on the former Glasgow, Dumbarton and Helensburgh line was replaced with the new Singer Station. At that time, the quite separate Kilbowie Road Station (seen here), which lay on the former Lanarkshire and Dumbartonshire line, was renamed Kilbowie Station. Until its closure on 5 October 1964, this was the most central of Clydebank's five stations and was accessed by steps on Kilbowie Road at Rosebery Place. For many years, a beautifully decorated Christmas tree was sited at the station entrance. In the late 1970s, the station was finally demolished, and the site cleared and landscaped. Also in this picture are some of the old tenements that once stood on Binnie Place (on the left) and Alexander Street (on the right). All of these tenements were demolished in the 1970s to make way for the new Clyde Shopping Centre.

Clydebank Bowling Club (initially Clydebank Bowling and Quoiting Club) was established in September 1884 at a site in John Knox Street. The site was bought from Miss Grace Hamilton of Barns by James Rodger Thomson, one of the proprietors of the nearby Clydebank Shipyard. Its first clubhouse had been built around 1886 and, being fairly small in size, all social events were held either in the adjacent Clydebank Public Hall, or in nearby Elgin Street School. When the much larger clubhouse, seen here, was eventually built, the smaller one was used for storage. The new clubhouse, which was designed by Robert Carswell of Yoker and cost almost £2,000 to build, was described in a *Glasgow Evening Times* article of the time as a 'unique and handsome structure having no equal in Great Britain as a bowling pavilion'. It was officially opened, using a specially engraved silver key, on 4 May 1907 by David McGhee, the manager of Clydebank Shipyard.

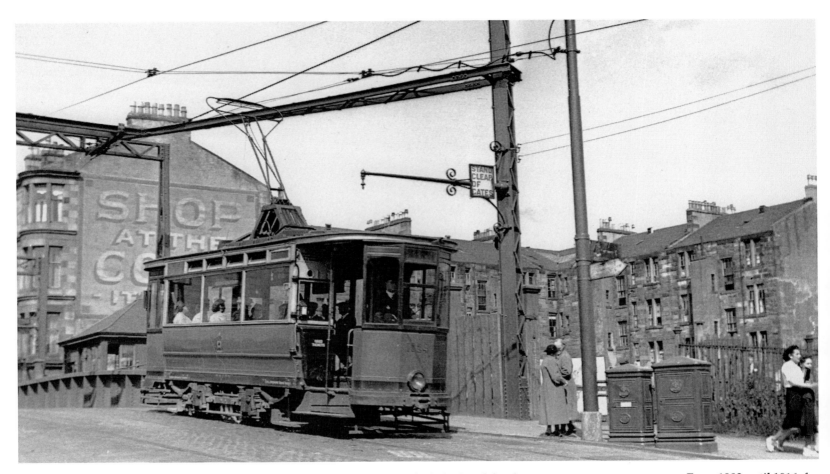

Over the years this stretch of Kilbowie Road, where it crosses the Forth and Clyde Canal, has been no stranger to controversy. From 1903 until 1916, for example, the question of who should pay towards the cost of a new metal swing bridge to replace the old wooden bascule bridge (seen here) was a matter of great dispute between the Canal owners, Glasgow Corporation and Clydebank Burgh Council. The matter was not resolved until the new bridge was opened. Another controversy, which occurred in 1960, centred on the rather innocuous gable end seen here bearing the slogan 'Shop at the Co-op'. Traditionally, this gable end had been used for advertisements. However, despite the presence of an existing (albeit very faint) poster, and traffic on the bridge being restricted to a speed of 10 m.p.h., the Council refused permission for the erection of an advertising hoarding, citing road safety. This eventually led to a public inquiry, from which the Council emerged victorious.

Rossdhu Place, seen here on the right opposite Singer's Buildings, was once home to two popular Clydebank hostelries – the Kilbowie Bar and the Rossdhu Bar. The latter, at the corner of Livingstone Street, was the second public house to be opened by former Dalmuir farmer, Andrew McGown, who had started his business with money received from the Lanarkshire and Dumbartonshire Railway Company in compensation for the loss of his Dalmuir Farm. He later went into partnership with Dugald Cameron to form McGown and Cameron Limited. After Andrew McGown's death in 1933, the business continued under the stewardship of Dugald Cameron until his death in 1951. Around 1968, both public houses were served with Compulsory Purchase Orders in preparation for the building of the new Clyde Shopping Centre, and they finally closed on 1 November 1973. Also in this picture, in the far distance at the entrance to Graham Street, can be seen one of the twin domes of the Palace Theatre. The Palace began its life in 1905 as an eating establishment, but before 1913 was converted into a variety theatre and renamed Cinem Varieties.

By the 1930s, when this aerial view was taken, Singer's Kilbowie factory had spread well beyond the 46 acres initially earmarked for the production of its sewing machines and accessories. Although Singer and Clydebank are now synonymous, if it hadn't been for the obstinacy of one particular person, this might not have been the case! Originally, Singer had chosen a site in Bonnybridge, Stirlingshire, for their new factory. A particular advantage of that site was its close proximity to George Ure and Company's foundry, which at that time supplied all the castings for Singer sewing machines. However, one landowner refused to sell his ground to Singer, forcing the company to proceed with their second option – the site at Kilbowie. This was reasonably near Singer's existing factory in Glasgow, and also benefited from being beside a main railway line and a canal. The first turf was cut on 18 May 1882 and, as they say, the rest is history! In February 1981, shortly after the Kilbowie factory was closed, the site was largely cleared to allow the construction of the new Clydebank Business Park to proceed.

In this view, taken *c*.1911, Singer workers are seen leaving the factory by the Kilbowie Road exit – probably heading for the trains at Singer Lye. The Lye was little more than a series of railway platforms, which had been constructed by the North British Railway specifically for Singer workers. It was built to ease congestion at Singer Station which was, at that time, unable to cope with the volume of passengers at peak times. This volume was not, however, solely due to Singer workers – by the late 1890s, as many as five railway stations, in addition to special workers' platforms, were required to cope with the daily movement of thousands of workers to and from Clydebank. This was claimed at the time to be unique in Scotland: Singer workers alone needed up to fourteen special trains between 6 a.m. and 7 a.m. The demand resulted in Singer workers reputedly benefiting from the cheapest fares on the North British Railway network. Unfortunately, although the fares were low, the carriages provided were very basic – in fact, workers brought their own candles to provide light!

This view shows Singer workers leaving the factory by the north gate on Second Avenue. Around 1906, the Singer Manufacturing Company embarked on a series of alterations to the original 1884 factory. Some of these alterations can be seen in this early view of the factory. They include the addition of a further two floors to the two Main Buildings (which incorporated the Singer clock tower). These Main Buildings (seen here to the rear of the two-storey offices on the left) comprised two parallel blocks each 800 feet long by 50 feet wide. Behind the six-storey Engineering block (seen here to the right of the offices) is the six-storey-high Cabinet Department. This was completed in 1904 in the astonishing time of six months. It measured 800 feet long by 80 feet wide and, by coincidence, was approximately equal to the length and breadth of the ill-fated John Brown-built passenger liner, *Lusitania*.

In this 1907 view of Kilbowie Road, looking north towards the Kilbowie Hill, the most prominent building is the red sandstone tenement opposite the North British Railway's Singer Station. Known locally as Bannerman Place, this tenement was built around the turn of the last century. Until its demolition in the late 1970s, shops and businesses occupied all of the ground-floor premises. The near corner shop, for example, was for many years occupied by the Clydebank Co-operative Society's No. 16 Grocery Department. By the late 1920s, the Society had opened further shops in Bannerman Place, including Fleshing and Dairy Departments. Directly above the Grocery Department was S. Mitchell's (later B.W. Shearer's) Dental Surgery. Other businesses located here included the Royal Billiard Saloon, the New Kinema Picture House, Thomas Ness (stationer) and the popular Singer Café. The café was owned by the Tedeschi family, who also owned the Regal Café at the foot of Kilbowie Road, beside the Clydebank Bar.

The 'Holy City', seen here *c.*1906, was laid out between 1904 and 1907 by Robert McAlpine and Sons. The development consisted of three parallel curving terraces of flat-roofed houses which, from a distance, were said to resemble Jerusalem, hence the name. These houses were erected on Kilbowie Hill to the north of Singer's Kilbowie Factory and, when built, were outwith the Clydebank Burgh boundary. When Radnor Park was absorbed into Clydebank Burgh in 1906, the houses were thought not to meet the more stringent local building standards then in force, but despite this they continued to be inhabited. Not surprisingly, when an attempt was made to raise rents in the early 1920s, the Holy City became a key battleground in the fight to retain existing rent levels. The Holy City was largely destroyed during the Clydebank Blitz. The little that remained was demolished in the 1960s during redevelopment of the area.

In late June 1906, contractors Robert McAlpine and Sons began levelling land immediately to the south of the 'Holy City' (seen here on higher ground above Singer Station). Their object was to divert a short stretch of the North British Railway's Glasgow, Dumbarton and Helensburgh line, in order to release ground for the Singer Manufacturing Company to expand their Kilbowie Factory. This short diversion commenced some 200 yards to the east of the old Kilbowie Station (which at that time was located to the east of Kilbowie Road) before rejoining the original railway line further to the west. As part of an agreement with Singer, the North British Railway agreed to replace their original Kilbowie Station with the new station seen here. This was named Singer Station and was one of only two stations in Britain to be named after a commercial enterprise. It was opened on 3 November 1907 and, if newspaper reports of the day are to be believed, was a marked improvement on the original Kilbowie Station, which they described as having been a 'dingy, woe-begone, sad-looking antiquated place'!

The Bannerman Street tenements (seen here *c.*1912), located to the rear of Bannerman Place, were built around 1900. Apart from the sweetie shops on Kilbowie Road, the most popular local venue for the Bannerman Street kids was undoubtedly the New Kinema picture house, the rear emergency entrance of which opened onto Bannerman Street. This cinema, more popularly known as the 'Kinch' or 'bug house', opened in 1914. Although its basic wooden seating was originally a constant cause for complaint, patrons could later upgrade to plusher (but inevitably more expensive) upholstered velvet tip-up seats. In the 1930s, the New Kinema was converted for 'talkies', but by the late 1940s it had fallen into disuse. It later re-opened as the Clyde Cinema and, by 1950, was in the ownership of the Pennycook Cinema Circuit. In October 1952, the cinema was given a six-month reprieve from closure by Clydebank Town Council, to allow necessary and expensive repairs to be carried out. However, these never came to fruition and the cinema closed down in 1953.

At one time it was said that it seemed there was a public house on almost every street corner in Clydebank, and this early 1940s view of Clydebank Cross shows two of these. On the left is Hutcheon's Clydebank Bar, and on the right is T.F. Ross's public house (later the Seven Seas). The Ross family were in business in Clydebank for almost 90 years and are said to have held the town's first liquor licence, as well as having opened Clydebank's first shop. This was situated within Clydebank Shipyard and reputedly sold everything from needles to anchors! Other well-established businesses at the Cross included Leslie Kirk (painter and decorator), Callaghan's confectioners (which sold 'assortments to suit every palate from the homely Imperial – solace of the older generation – to the daintily boxed Chocolate'), and a branch of R.S. McColl's confectionery chain. When R.S. McColl's opened here in February 1915, they advertised such delicacies as 'Russian toffee, treacle toffee, cream caramels and peppermint lumps'.

Despite some infilling at the foot of Kilbowie Hill in 1906, in an endeavour to lessen the steepness of the incline, climbing the Hill (as it was more familiarly known) was still a daunting task for the largely horse-drawn traffic that negotiated it on a daily basis. Sometimes the incline proved just too formidable, as happened in January 1907, when a butcher's cart capsized giving, it was said, stray dogs 'an excellent opportunity to secure a feed'! Some 20 years later it was still proving difficult – this time for trainee drivers on the Glasgow Corporation tramway route to Duntocher. In fact, the steepness of Kilbowie Road was such that trams on this route were the first in the Corporation's fleet to be fitted with air brakes – to prevent them from rolling backwards downhill. It is said that instructors would test the mettle of trainee drivers by allowing the trams to run freely down the Hill and then gauging the drivers' reactions. One report suggests that several drivers lost their nerve and bailed out into the middle of the road!

At one time, Radnor Park was a shoppers' paradise, boasting over a hundred shops. These included sixteen grocers, fifteen confectioners, eleven dairies, ten newsagents, two post offices and a bank. In this view of Kilbowie Hill, taken *c*.1910, some of these shops can be seen within the tenements on the left. They include, Cameron (butcher), George Robertson (chemist), John Wilson (barber) and, from numbers 295 to 303, a suite of Clydebank Co-operative Society departments. Beyond Graham Avenue (the first opening on the left) was Thomas Capaldi's ice cream shop, Miss Annie Mills' shoe shop, and a further Clydebank Co-operative Society department. Sadly, all of these businesses were lost when the tenements were destroyed during the Clydebank Blitz. Afterwards the site was cleared, but for many years it lay derelict, prompting one local resident in the mid-1960s to comment that the site might be one of the few 'war ravaged' areas still to be found in Britain.

Radnor Street or, as it was formerly known, Skypes Road, was one of the first streets in the Radnor Park area to be laid out. It ran a distance of several miles, from Kilbowie Road in the east to Boquhanran Road in the west. The first houses were erected here around 1885 by J.W. Anderson, a retired Glasgow businessman. He had purchased the ground in Skypes Road in order to erect workmen's houses. He was followed in 1904 by a local contractor, Leslie Kirk, who acquired land on which to build tenements. These tenements (some of which can be seen here alongside McCallum's public house, on the far left) were largely destroyed during the Clydebank Blitz. On the far right is a Clydebank Co-operative Society shop. Until 1908, when Clydebank Co-operative Society and Radnor Park Co-operative Society merged, these two societies were bitter rivals. The rivalry was intensified in 1902, when Clydebank Co-operative Society opened a suite of shops in Radnor Street.

All of the properties seen here (including Tennent's public house at the corner of Radnor Street and Robertson Street) were destroyed during the Clydebank Blitz. Regrettably, the wholesale destruction of the Radnor Park area during the Blitz marked the break-up of a community once renowned for its fierce independence and strong co-operative spirit. Many 'Radnorians' (as the residents of Radnor Park were once called) achieved a measure of fame in various walks of life, none more so than the Antarctic explorer, Captain Andrew Laidlaw Nelson. In an outstanding naval career Nelson, who was educated at nearby Boquhanran School, took part in three expeditions to the South Pole. During one of these expeditions in 1930, and while a lieutenant aboard the research ship *Discovery I*, he steered his vessel through a strait in the South Atlantic which now bears his name. Another famous Radnorian was John Gardner, who went under the name of Ronnie Genarder. Although perhaps now little heard of, Gardner was in his time regarded by some as Britain's first crooner, and was known as the 'British Bing Crosby'.

By 1911, when this photograph was taken, the area around Clydebank Cross was sufficiently congested to merit the daily presence of a policeman to control both pedestrian and vehicular traffic. In the main, this congestion was due to the large numbers of workers and shoppers who frequented the many shops, banks and dining establishments located at and around the Cross. Among the more popular businesses here were Watt's and Sibbald's (both drapers and outfitters). Sibbald's, who opened premises nearby at the corner of Glasgow Road and Somerville Street in December 1903, was then advertising, amongst other things, a comprehensive range of half-price ladies' morning gowns for 3s. 11d. each. Also at the Cross was T.F. Ross's public bar (extreme left of picture in Victoria Place). Yet another public house, the equally popular Duntocher Bar, was located almost directly opposite on the south side of Glasgow Road, just to the east of Somerville Street.

Before the opening of the Town Hall in 1902, Clydebank's Chambers and Administrative Offices were housed in the Glasgow Road tenements on the far left. The premises were actually a double-fronted shop and it is said that interested citizens wishing to follow Council proceedings could stand outside the Chambers with their ears pressed to the window! In late 1920, a Clydebank branch of the City Bakeries chain was opened within this same shop. Initially, it consisted simply of a baker's shop, but later a tea-room and a function suite (jointly known as the Windsor Rooms) were added. Access to the Windsor Rooms, which were situated above the shop, was by way of a set of stairs to the left of the shop frontage on Glasgow Road. The tea-room quickly became a popular venue for busy shoppers, who regularly popped in for a morning or afternoon 'cuppa', or to sample the 'high teas' for which the tea-room was justly famous. In October 1973, despite fierce protests from loyal customers, the popular Windsor Rooms were closed by the owners.

The vibrancy of this 1960s view of Glasgow Road is sure to bring back fond memories to generations of local shoppers. Among the many long-standing businesses in this area were (at the corner of Alexander Street) William Marshall's shoe shop and Claude Alexander the tailors. Undoubtedly, however, one of the biggest attractions for local shoppers was F.W. Woolworth, which was situated at the corner of Glasgow Road and Wallace Street. Known to the company as Store No. 759, it was a distinctive white-tiled art deco building with red and gold signage. When it opened in 1939 it proved to be an immediate hit with local shoppers, who referred to it as the 'sixpenny store' since no item cost more than sixpence. The first floor of the building housed, besides a stock room, the staff canteen. Here at one time a shilling would buy staff a lunch of soup, mince and potatoes, and a cup of tea – out of their then weekly wage of £4 (80 shillings). In 1982, a few years after the store closed, the premises were re-opened as the Lucky Break Snooker Club.

Alexander Street was laid out in the early 1880s. In May 1885, Clydebank Co-operative Society opened the premises shown here. Initially there were two shops at ground level, and fifteen houses on the ground and upper levels. The shops included a Fleshing Department and a Drapery and Hardware Department. The latter department in particular proved such a success that, within a few years of its opening, the Society was obliged to consider larger premises. Eventually, in 1894, members were given the option of either building an extension onto the existing premises or converting one of the fifteen houses. In the event, the conversion was agreed. Around the same time, a further ground-floor house was converted into a Boot and Shoe Department. In 1903, the Society converted all the remaining ground-floor houses for use as shops.

In the late 1800s, despite intense competition from other local grocers such as Aitken, Leckie and Massey, the Clydebank Co-operative Society's grocery shops prospered. The first, which was located at the corner of Glasgow Road and Canal Street and sold groceries, butcher meat, fruit and vegetables, was open for an amazing 70 hours a week. Their first employee was a former Glasgow grocer, James McKie. He was appointed on a weekly wage of £1. 10s. and was required to deposit a security of £20 to the Society. His working day was from 8.00 a.m. until 7.30 p.m., with a half-hour break for breakfast and an hour for lunch. Within a week of taking up the post, Mr McKie protested at the long hours and, in particular, the shortness of his early morning breaks. The Society's response was to suggest that, instead of closing the shop for breakfast, he ate this on the premises. Not surprisingly, Mr McKie only lasted two months with the Society!

When it was first built, Clydebank Terrace on Glasgow Road was designed to provide living accommodation for Clydebank Shipyard workers. Each house was fairly basic, being made up of two rooms and a kitchen. These houses were in complete contrast to the more salubrious Atlas Cottages which were built further east on Glasgow Road many years later in 1916, to house shipyard foremen. Around 1900 local house factors George Paterson and Sons (who were themselves located within Clydebank Terrace until 1967) were authorised by the yard to begin letting out the ground-floor properties for commercial purposes, with it being allowed that 'shops could be constructed in this property to suit tenants' needs'. One of the first businesses to take advantage of the scheme was James Nelson and Sons (butchers). Another was Alexander Massey and Sons (provision merchants), who opened a shop at No. 62. This well-stocked shop, seen here around 1907, clearly prospered, for some seven decades later in 1973 they were still in business in these same premises.

In its heyday, this stretch of Glasgow Road from Clydebank Cross to Brown's gate boasted a number of shops. Many of Clydebank's longest established businesses were located here. These included John McChleary (shoe shop), James McCulloch (tobacconist and newsagent), Alexander Aitken (grocer and tea merchant), and Francis Spite and Company (chemist). A popular venue also in this area was the Restaurant in Belmont Place. Better known as Connelly's Bar, it was contained within the second tenement from the right of the picture, and was one of Clydebank's best-known public houses. It was used by generations of John Brown workers and, in addition to serving food and drink, was at one time more of a meeting place: it was here that shipyard squads would 'divvy' out their wages, outstanding debts would be settled, and news and gossip exchanged. After Dan Connelly's death, long-serving manager Dennis McLaughlin took over the running of the bar on behalf of the Connelly family. By then Connelly's Bar had become an institution and had even featured in two national television documentaries.

This view of Glasgow Road was taken from the corner of North and South Elgin Street (to the right and left respectively) around 1907. At the corner of North Elgin Street is the Theatre Café. This proved to be well placed for patrons of the Gaiety Theatre, the main entrance of which was almost directly opposite. After the Gaiety re-opened as the Bank Cinema in November 1927, with a new entrance on Glasgow Road, the Theatre Café's popularity declined, being eclipsed by the Bank Café, which had opened alongside the cinema. Other long-established businesses on this stretch of Glasgow Road included the Emporium, J. Docherty (butcher), William Colquhoun (dairy), C. Roxburgh (sweet shop), Florence (or Flossie) Freil (confectioner and grocer), and Margaret Gray (newsagent, stationer and tobacconist). Margaret Gray stocked a wide range of goods, including Dr Plum and Irwin pipes, Biro pens, and Bestway and Weldon's fashion books and knitting leaflets. In the far distance can be seen the spire of St James' Church.

Clydebank Terrace, seen here to the west of the Clydebank Shipyard gate, was one of the first housing properties to be built in Clydebank. Erected in 1872 by J. and G. Thomson for their workers (and thus more commonly known as Thomson's Buildings), it stood on Glasgow Road and comprised two blocks of four-storey tenements. Within these were 126 houses (consisting of two rooms and a kitchen each), which could accommodate a total of 700 people. Later, when some of the ground-floor properties were converted into shops, long-established businesses such as John R. Taylor (drapers) moved in. This busy drapery (known locally as the Red House) specialised in overalls and boiler suits for the shipyard workers and had been established by John's father, Thomas. It was originally located in premises at the corner of Glasgow Road and Canal Street (which were later occupied by the *Evening Times*). In 1953, John Brown and Company were given permission to renovate part of the Terrace which had lain derelict since the Clydebank Blitz. However, in late 1978 all of the tenements seen here were demolished.

In earlier years, one of the attractions for holidaymakers 'going doon the watter' was the view of ships under construction in the various shipyards between the Broomielaw and Greenock. On this occasion, the holidaymakers on the Denny-built paddle steamer *Caledonia* must have been delighted with the view, for in the Clydebank Shipyard is one of a series of four beautiful Cunarders being finished off in the fitting-out basin. These vessels, the *Saxonia*, *Ivernia*, *Carinthia* and *Sylvania*, were built between 1954 and 1956 for the Liverpool-based Cunard shipping company. The paddle steamer itself had been launched from William Denny's Dumbarton yard in 1934, entering service in 1935 for the Caledonian Steam Packet Company to ferry passengers between Gourock, Wemyss Bay and Largs. In 1939, PS *Caledonia* had been requisitioned for wartime minesweeping duties and her name changed to HMS *Goatfell*. After de-commissioning in 1945, she resumed her previous role. She was withdrawn from service in 1969 and later bought by brewers Bass Charrington for use as a floating pub on the River Thames.

Before the laying down of SS *Lusitania*'s keel in August 1904, the eight existing berths within the East Yard at Clydebank had been reduced to six to cope with the bigger ships then being built. The *Lusitania* was assigned berth No. 4. The eventual launch of this giant passenger liner was carried out on 7 June 1906 by Lady Inverclyde. The ceremony was witnessed by a record crowd of spectators, including some 7,500 Brown's workers, who had been given a day's holiday for the occasion. The following year, this passenger liner (the world's first 30,000-ton vessel) was guided downriver by six tugs to begin her sea trials. With the exception of a moment's anxiety when, whilst negotiating Bowling Bay, the liner strayed a little too close to the north bank, her passage downriver went smoothly. She was handed over to Cunard on 26 August 1907, and began her maiden voyage to New York on 7 September 1907. On 7 May 1915, following a short but distinguished career, the *Lusitania* was sunk off the coast of Ireland by a German U-boat.

In 1907, Clydebank Shipyard invested in a massive 150-ton cantilever crane, seen here alongside the fitting-out basin. This had become necessary as they were starting to build much larger ships. As well as being one of the very first of its type to be supplied to a UK shipyard, it was for many years by far the largest crane in the shipyard. It was designed and built by the Glasgow firm, Sir William Arrol and Company. Afterwards, as ships were becoming larger still, further large cranes were erected. In 1989, in an attempt to secure its future, the crane shown here was given a Category B listing by Historic Scotland. By late April 2002 it was one of only three large cranes left standing in Clydebank Shipyard. Shortly thereafter, first one crane, then another were toppled, leaving only this crane standing. Also in the picture (at the right) can be seen the pole derricks and 120-ton sheerleg cranes which the yard also used – the former for light weights and the latter for heavy weights.

Opposite: In 1950, the former North British Chemical Works, which stood on the south bank of the Forth and Clyde Canal at Whitecrook, were leased to John Brown Landboilers. A division of John Brown and Company, this company manufactured land boilers for UK power stations. At that time, the derelict chemical works buildings (or 'seaweed factory' as it was locally known) were demolished and the West or 'Big' Shed erected in their place. This shed was a massive structure and was used by John Brown Landboilers until 1964, when the company (by then Foster Wheeler John Brown) relocated downriver to the former Denny Shipyard in Dumbarton. In 1974 the West Shed was again put to use – on this occasion by the newly formed John Brown Engineering Offshore for the manufacture of modules and other structures for North Sea oil installations. After the closure of John Brown Engineering Offshore in 1978, the West Shed was largely used for storage, until Thor Ceramics (now RHI Refactories) took over the site in 1986.

JOHN BROWN & Cº (CLYDEBANK) LIMITED

WHITECROOK WORKS

CLYDEBANK

PHONE. CLYDEBANK 2441

The Bisley Buildings (properly Bisley Place) were erected by the late 1890s at latest and stood on Glasgow Road, at the corner of North Elgin Street. Prominent in this view (taken around 1914) is Mac's Royal Restaurant. This restaurant was run by Peter McGibbon from around 1898, and continued to be run by his widow, Jessie, well into the 1920s. The restaurant was later renamed the Bisley Bar. In the 1950s, the area around the bar was known as the 'Bisley corner' and became the haunt of the locally infamous 'Bisley Boys' – a notorious gang of local youths. Other businesses located here over time included John Carruth (baker), a billiards hall and Todd's School of Dancing. At one time Clydebank's leading dancing school, Todd's occupied much of the second floor of the Buildings. Around the corner in North Elgin Street stood Clydebank's first purpose-built theatre, the Gaiety, which opened on Monday 27 January 1902.

In 1903 William Hall, then already the proprietor of a successful laundry in Dunoon, opened a new facility in Barns Street, Clydebank. This newly built laundry (seen here on the right) adjoined Clydebank East Station. It was one of the first buildings to be erected in this area, which would later become known as Whitecrook. Built of brick, it had an area of 10,000 square feet and was fitted out with all the latest laundry equipment, which had been supplied and installed by James Ritchie's Glenavon Works in Partick. The laundry was officially opened on 29 July 1903 by Provost Alexander Stewart. At the opening ceremony, it was suggested by Mr Ritchie that Mr Hall might later care to 'invite the ladies of the district to look over the premises'. From the start, the laundry offered a door-to-door collection service, which was hugely popular but which was discontinued in 1966, because the laundry could no longer cope with the demand. Unfortunately, the laundry was less successful in its later years and finally, in November 1974, it was closed by its then owners, Bowie-Castlebank.

The 'jewel in the crown' of the 201-acre Whitecrook Open Space was a large purpose-built model yachting pond. Built by the Town Council at a cost of £5,000 using unemployed labour, the pond was officially opened on 25 April 1925 by the Provost, Samuel MacDonald. Immediately after the opening, the Fleet Commodore for the day (who was the Council's Sanitary Inspector, R.D. Brown) signalled the start of a mini-regatta featuring 30 model yachts. However, following a mid-pool collision with several yachts, a steam-driven model liner (which had apparently escaped without any damage) suddenly and dramatically listed to the side and quickly sank, bow first, in the two feet of water – much to the amusement of the spectators. Beside the pond a rockery had been laid out using between 70 and 80 tons of rock. For a number of years, Clydebank Model Yachting Club held their meetings at the pond, but by the 1970s the pond had largely fallen into disuse.

For many years, Bankies were uplifted by the sound of drums and tambourines when the Salvation Army held their regular Saturday evening open-air Witness Meetings. These took place at the corner of Glasgow Road and Alexander Street. Afterwards, the band would march back to their Citadel in Alexander Street. The Clydebank Corps was formed in 1893 as an outpost of the Whiteinch Corps. Within five years they had formed their own band (seen here outside their original Citadel) under Bandmaster Joe Wilson. Joe was succeeded in 1915 by James Borthwick, who led the band until 1961. When it was first formed, there were only twelve bandsmen, but it very quickly established itself as one of the leading Salvation Army bands in Scotland. At the opening of a new Citadel in 1929 (on the site of the old Citadel), the band took part in the opening service. More recently, they played at a special concert held in Clydebank Town Hall on 20 June 1998 to mark their centenary.

By 1898, the level of coal and mineral ore imports coming into the Clyde was such that the Clyde Trustees were obliged to construct a new dock with specialised berths and quay space. This was built on the site of the former Napier, Shanks and Bell shipyard at Clydebank. On 25 April 1907, the new Rothesay Dock was officially opened by the Prince and Princess of Wales, who sailed into the dock on board the Clydebank-built paddle steamer *Duchess of Rothesay*, in the process cutting a purple ribbon which was stretched across the dock entrance. Provost John Taylor presented the Prince of Wales with a scroll enclosed in a silver casket decorated with gold. The Princess of Wales was then presented with a beautiful vase filled with wine, some of which she poured onto a memorial stone to name the dock. The Prince used an ivory mallet to 'tap' the memorial stone, thus signifying the official opening of the dock.

The new Rothesay Dock had cost £578,889 to build and was largely completed within seven years of the cutting of the first sod on 13 August 1900. When opened, it was one of the most up-to-date docks in Britain. The 735-foot-long inner basin (seen here) was accessed from a 200-foot-wide outer entrance, and was wide enough to allow vessels of up to 600 feet in length to operate within it. By 1911, the dock was fully equipped with cranes, hoists and railway sidings, and was capable of handling sixteen ships simultaneously. In this view, the Nos. 1 and 2 coal hoists can be seen on the left, on either side of the brick-built Generating Station. On the opposite side of the dock, several travelling cranes and a transporter can be seen.

Although most of the railway structures seen here were demolished after the line closed in 1964, the ornate red brick and sandstone Clydebank Riverside Station (seen here on the left) has survived. Designed by Sir J.J. Burnet, it was built around 1896. The station was one of several on the Lanarkshire and Dumbartonshire Railway Company line, which had been built primarily to serve the docks and riverside industries on the north bank of the River Clyde. Just to the west of the station the line turned sharply north, following the old filled-in bed of the Forth and Cart Junction Canal. Although initially the line was very popular, it was in its final years used almost solely by John Brown workers. The station, which is situated to the rear of the Atlas Cottages, between Clyde Street and Cunard Street, was listed in 1984 and converted into flats in 1994.

On 25 August 1978, demolishers began the task of pulling down St James' Church on Glasgow Road. This church (seen here alongside the former British Linen Bank building) was Clydebank's oldest church. It had its origins in a workers' bothy in Clydebank Shipyard. Because of its tar roof, the bothy became known as the 'Tarry Kirk', and it was said that during inclement weather worshippers had to use umbrellas to keep dry due to the nature of the roof! Services had initially been conducted on an informal basis by the Rev. Robert Henderson of Old Kilpatrick Parish Church, but in 1872 attendance was such that it was agreed a formal preaching station should be established in the bothy. Under the enthusiastic guidance of the new minister, the Rev. J.H. Pringle, plans were soon put in place for a permanent church on Glasgow Road. The foundation stone of the new church was laid in August 1875 by Miss Grace Hamilton, the local benefactress who had been involved at the inception of Clydebank, and the church opened on 19 November 1876.

Separated from St Columba's Episcopal Church by a tenement block, which was known locally as 'purgatory', was Our Holy Redeemer's Church. This church opened on Glasgow Road in 1903 and replaced an earlier, and much smaller Chapel School, the front gable and roof of which can just be glimpsed on the far right of the picture. Beyond the church, at the corner of South Bank Street, stood Peter Halket's Blythswood Bar. Further along still, at 300 Glasgow Road, was one of Clydebank's most prestigious hairdressing salons, run by Henry Liverani, whose most famous 'soap-boy' or apprentice was his son Julius. Winner of many awards, including the Grand Prix (World Championship Modern Hair Styling) trophy in 1946 and 1947, Julius was advertised at one time as being 'the world's leading hair stylist'. Not surprisingly, he was a favourite with celebrities, such as Sabrina, the glamorous 1950s film and television star. On the opposite side of Glasgow Road, at the corner of North Bank Street, was Stevie Scott's restaurant. This was at one time well patronised at lunchtime by pupils from Our Holy Redeemer's School, buying 'half dinners' (i.e., a starter and main course only).

This view of Glasgow Road was taken in 1934. The front elevation of Our Holy Redeemer's Primary School can just be glimpsed beyond Our Holy Redeemer's Church. Sadly, the primary school burned down in April 1973. In 1980, a new Our Holy Redeemer's Primary School was opened on East Barns Street. The ivy-covered grey sandstone block of houses on the far right, situated at the corner of North Bank Street, is Barns Place. In the late 1880s Father Peter Evers, the first parish priest of Our Holy Redeemer's, took up residence here. Another well-known local resident around this period was Alexander Aitken, a grocer and provision merchant. For many years the cottage with the steeply pitched roof adjacent to Barns Place was the residence of Betty McGhee, whose family owned several local public houses.

In 1895, a Chapel School was opened on Glasgow Road, to replace a smaller one opened six years earlier on Kilbowie Road. Initially, the classrooms within this new Chapel School were on the ground floor, with the chapel on the upper floor. However, in 1903 the whole of the building was converted for school use only, after the new Our Holy Redeemer's Church was opened alongside. Due to an ever-increasing school roll, a new annexe or 'middle school' (pictured here) was opened in 1913 in South Bank Street. At that time, the Glasgow Road school became the infants' school – known locally as the 'baby building'. In 1924, with even greater numbers of pupils, a further school annexe was opened in Clyde Street. Today, this is the only one of these three buildings which still stands.